STICKER STORIES
FIRE TRUCKS

illustrated by Edward Miller

Grosset & Dunlap
An Imprint of Penguin Group (USA) Inc.

ISBN 978-0-448-41825-4

Clang! Clang! goes the fire bell.
All the fire trucks are ready to go!
All the firefighters rush to hop on!

Here they come down the street.
Woo-ee! Woo-ee!

Lots of fire trucks
come to a big fire.

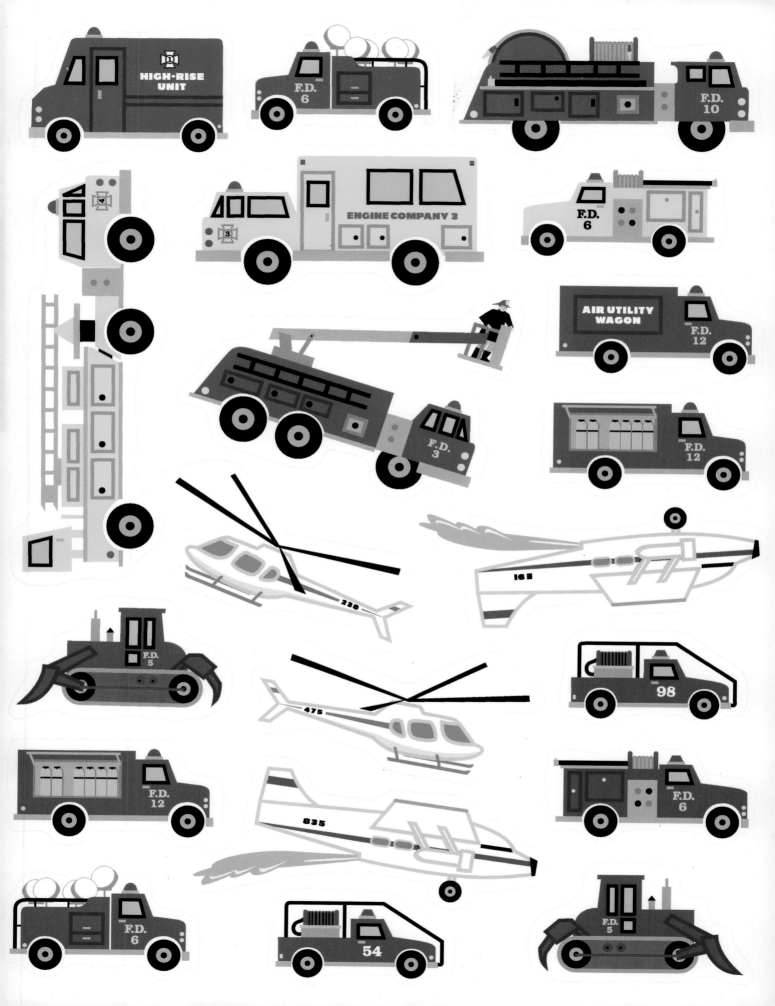

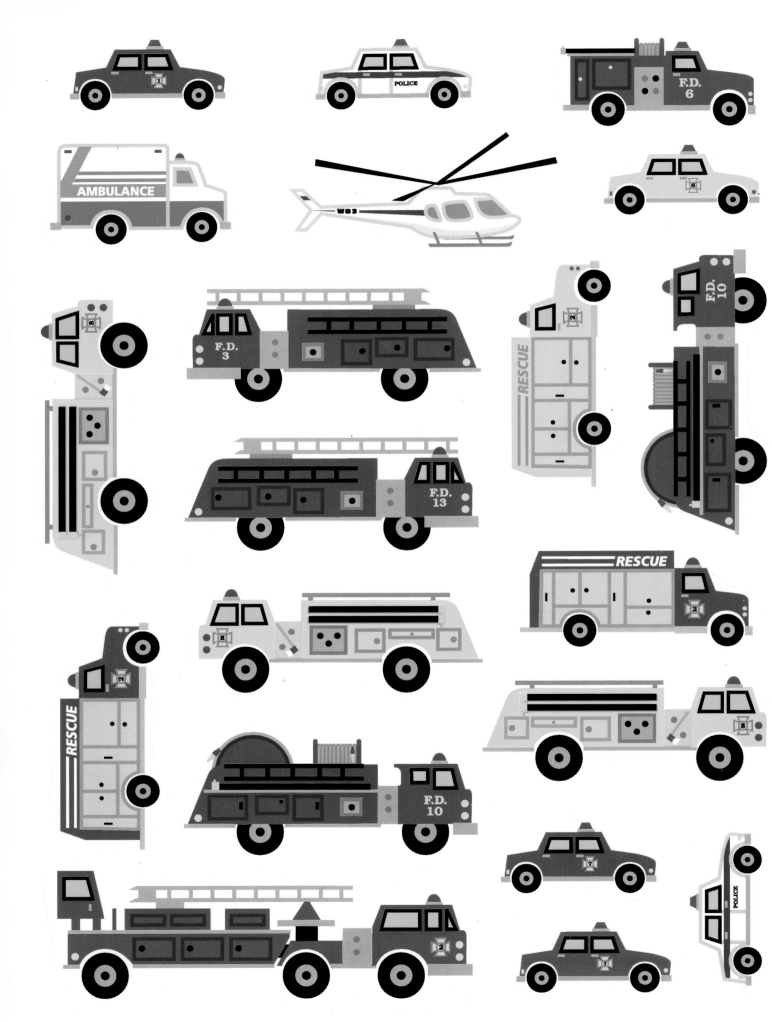

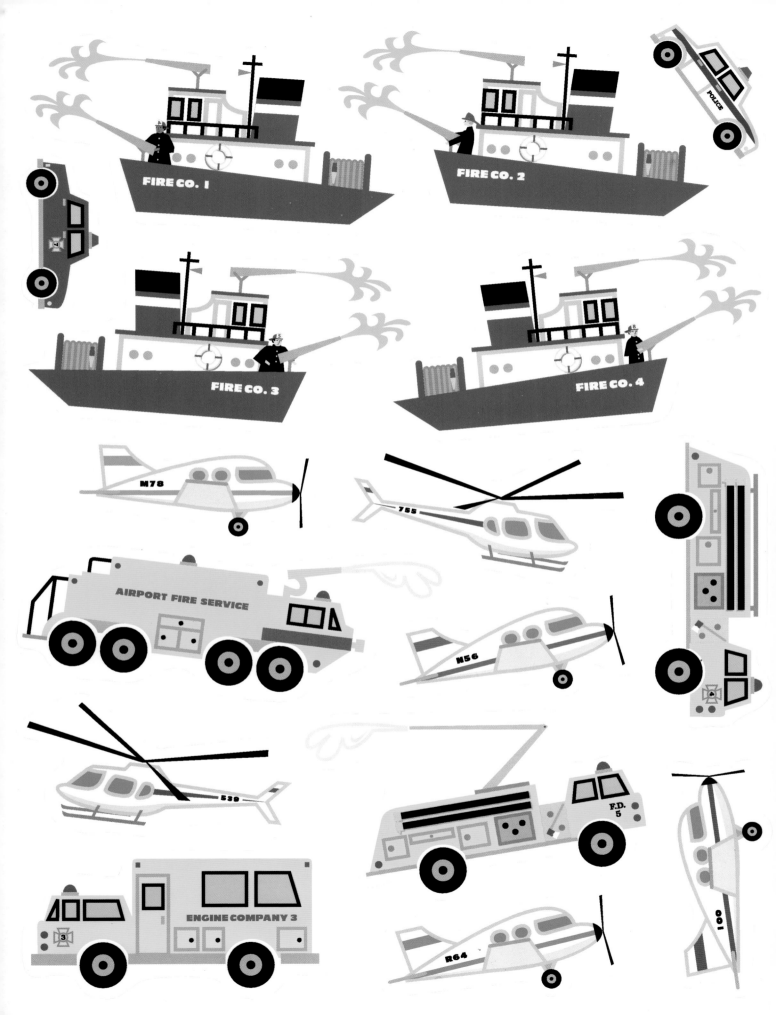

But when there's a forest fire,
ordinary fire trucks can't get through.
Bring in the bulldozers and brush trucks!
Send out the helicopters and airplanes!

When there's a fire out on the water,
fireboats race to the rescue!

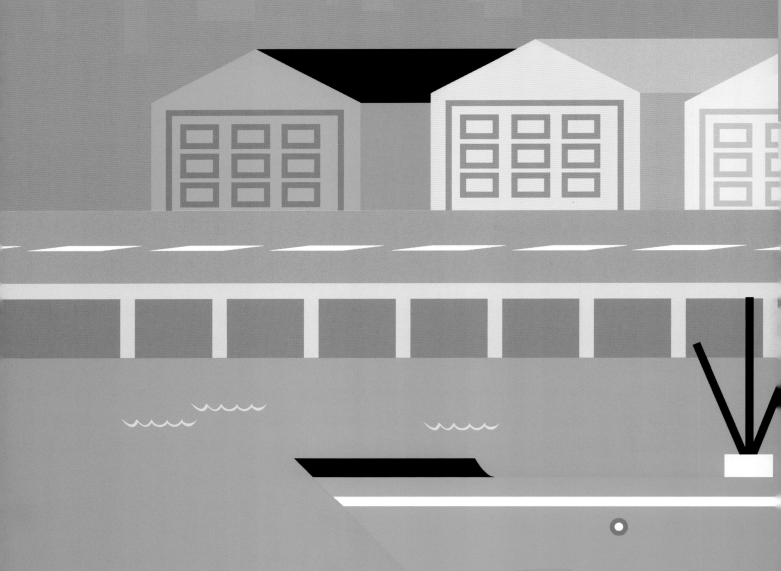

Firefighters have special equipment
for airport fires, too. Hurry!
Roll out the foam trucks
and spray on the foam!

Big fire or small fire—firefighters and fire trucks are there to help.

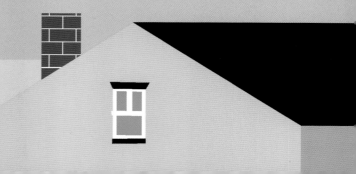

They help in lots of ways!